FROM THE STILL EMPTY GRAVE

WESTERN LITERATURE SERIES

A. WILBER STEVENS
FROM THE STILL EMPTY GRAVE

COLLECTED POEMS

Foreword by X. J. Kennedy

University of Nevada Press

Reno, Las Vegas & London

Western Literature Series Editor: John H. Irsfeld

A list of books in the series follows the index.

The paper used in this book meets the requirements of American National Standard for Information Sciences— Permanence of Paper for Printed Library Materials, ANSI Z39.48-1984. Binding materials were chosen for strength and durability.

Library of Congress Cataloging-in-Publication Data

Stevens, A. Wilber (Arthur Wilber), 1921–
From the still empty grave : collected poems / A. Wilber Stevens ; foreword by X. J. Kennedy.
p.   cm. — (Western literature series)
Includes index.
ISBN 0-87417-272-1 (paper ed.)
I. Title.   II. Series.
PS3569.T4395F76   1995
811'.54—dc20   95-16360
                                                          CIP

University of Nevada Press, Reno, Nevada 89557 USA
Copyright © 1995 University of Nevada Press
All rights reserved
Design by Robert Blesse
Printed in the United States of America

9 8 7 6 5 4 3 2 1

For my sons Arthur *Wilber* Stevens III
and Christopher Rivers Stevens
In memory of their mother,
Marjorie Rogers Stevens (1925–1979)

CONTENTS

Foreword   xi

ITINERARY OF LOST KNOWING

Itinerary of Lost Knowing   3
By the Malacca Straits   4
Sending Down   6
Postcard: Lamb House, Rue, East Sussex   7
Rye   8
Duet   9
Dead Birds   10
Another Poem on the Tearing Down of the
    Metropolitan Opera House   12
An Evening at Home   13
A Problem of Vision   15
Doors   16

BROOKLYN AND BROWN

A Particular Tenure   21
For Montgomery Clift   22

SEATTLE

For a Friend: Upon His Retiring to the Country
    Following a War   25
Visiting Poet   26
For the Least Ones   27
Critic Undefiled   29
On Drinking Guinness Stout: Seattle   30

IDAHO

The Wind of Hills   35
Idaho   36
Presence   37
If You Should Die   38
Here   39
Pocatello   40
Child Before Fire   48

BURMA

Christ in Burma   51
Burma: Nine Reflections on as Many Ferns   52
Mandalay   54
Blair in Burma   56
Earthquake: Burma   59
The World Is Going to End Up in Burma   61
Without Burma   62

BRAZIL

Maid: Brazil   65
The Sea Kicker (Rio)   66

ARIZONA

Insomnia from the Great Snow: Prescott   69
Today's Poet   71
For a Lady Poet Gone Bureaucrat   72
Wood Walk   73
The New Garden   74
Dress Informal   75
To Stop Smoking My Son Chewed   76

Purcell Afternoon   77
On Hearing the Choirboy Sing at a
    Stranger's Funeral   78
And One Other Thing   79
All Will Be Well in the Winter   80

MISSOURI

Calendar for Worship   83
Poem for My Son   84
Sleeper from Kansas City   85

LAS VEGAS

Vegas: A Few Scruples   89
My Dry Cleaner Branko Reads of the
    Shelling of Dubrovnik in the
    New York Times   90
Paradise Crest   91
Boy   92
Reading Pater in Las Vegas   93
Interval   94
Having It Made   95
To My Cat Drinking from the Swimming
    Pool   96
The Night Sammy Davis Jr. Couldn't Go On
    (Las Vegas)   97
Memorandum   98
The Failure of the Birds   99
Hearing the Voices   100
Cowboy Poetry Gathering: Elko   101
The Man with the Paper Hat   103
The Relay of the Cross   104

Journey   106
Arlen   109
Hands On   110

LETTER TO GREECE

Letter to Greece   113

Acknowledgments   117
Index of Titles and First Lines   119

FOREWORD

West is an idea of being away
So that one has to look at it from afar
                                    —"Arlen"

It is a curious fact of our literary life that, in order to
be considered a truly western poet, a poet is expected
to deliver tributes to rugged landscapes. Detailed evo-
cations of mountains, salt flats, canyons, and arroyos
will suffice; and the more desolate the regions he in-
spects, the more deeply rooted the poet is thought
to be. However, A. Wilber Stevens (the *A* stands for
Arthur, *Who's Who in America* tells us) is a western poet
like none other I know. True, he can write of the land,
in "Idaho,"

> I have heard the hills hurt and wonder,
> I have known water to cry and be afraid,
> I have seen boys and pebbles drag behind
> Thunder asking how to die alone and free.

But in those evocative lines, the hills and water
remain unspecified. The western landscapes that
Stevens most intently and knowingly describes are
urban or suburban ones, such as the Las Vegas Strip
in "Vegas: A Few Scruples" and a neighborhood of
householders in "Having It Made." In "To My Cat
Drinking from the Swimming Pool," he advises his
pet, "Take your chances indoors." I hesitate to pump
significance into that delectable bit of light verse, and

yet in his poetry Stevens seems generally to have followed that very advice. As some of his poems reveal, Stevens has also happened to live in a few exotic locales—Burma, Thailand, Brazil—and once coedited an anthology, *English Poetry by Indians*, published in Calcutta. Indeed, the present collection, as you can tell even from a cursory browse, has a wide and generously inclusive world-view.

Nonetheless, I see Stevens as clearly a westerner, by deliberate choice. He has traveled far from the coast where he was born (in Brooklyn) and went to college (Brown), for he appears to have taken Horace Greeley's classic counsel and headed westward to study and teach—to Washington (where he fell under the spell of poet Theodore Roethke), then to Idaho, Missouri, Arizona, Texas, and finally Nevada, where he has taught with distinction for more than twenty years.

What I would call his unmistakable westernness seems a matter of temperament: a certain impatience with fences and barriers, a defiant individuality. These attitudes might well be expected from a poet who, in a recent issue of *Interim*, editorially complained of a lack of chance-taking that he noticed in too many submitted stories and poems. Wistfully, he recalled certain wild and unkempt writers of the past, among them Henry Miller, whose contribution to the magazine Stevens had had to hitchhike out to Big Sur to obtain. "In those computerless days," he concluded, "some literature grew out of a miracle-hoping defiance rather than informed despair." Apparently,

Stevens enlisted on the side of defiance, both as poet and as editor. "I retch between prone steel and fixed ideas" he declares, and in "Another Poem on the Tearing Down of the Metropolitan Opera House" voices his sympathy for a crusty old baritone who once shook a fist at his audience.

Unwilling to settle for a safe and conventional course, Stevens takes dizzying risks. The reckless energy of certain of his poems reminds me of Dylan Thomas, whose failures are so often more memorable than the successes of his timid peers. If anything, Stevens at times aims higher than words can travel. Robert Browning might have approved: "A man's reach must exceed his grasp"—and so might William Faulkner, who found that kind of quixotic aspiration in only the greatest American writers. In "Pocatello," a longish sequence, Stevens seems to be trying to state the unstatable—to wrap words around the whole of his life and the whole extent of his feelings. Tall order. But I would urge the reader to accept Stevens's work on faith, for it is necessary to go along with his occasional excesses in order to reap his rewards. When Stevens takes a long chance and wins, he is unsurpassable, as in "Burma: Nine Reflections on as Many Ferns" with its wonderful conclusion, "Dying everywhere caressing all / I see the grass between your eyes."

Stevens, I must admit, doesn't always make life simple for us. Terse but richly ambiguous poems such as "Itinerary of Lost Knowing" and "A Particular Tenure" resist the mind *almost* successfully, and with each rereading invite new interpretations. These and other poems abound in lines that startle and oblige us to look twice:

> There was no moon when they left him
> He coughed and looned alone
> He shed his skin on an acre
> They couldn't feel the he of him
>
> A Saint can build a box kite with his sins
> And hold his shriven pity by a string
>
> God's ice is my only road.

I find myself learning those lines by heart, though unable to paraphrase them. But let me not dwell too long on Stevens's difficulties, for they are by no means discouraging. In truth, much of his work is plainspoken. Even a poem that, taken line by line, may pose difficulties—the splendid lyric, "Boy"—in its entirety makes clear its attitude of wonder and reverence. Like all poets whose work is worth rereading many times, Stevens defies the critic to translate his words into other, duller words. Whether clear at once or challenging, his lines often cry out to be quoted, for they arrange words in ways that could hardly be improved: "The mothers walk hurling the wind away."

For much of his career, Stevens has been involved with the poetry and fiction of other writers—lesser-known and struggling writers, as well as some of the most widely celebrated. Back in 1944 in Seattle he founded the literary magazine *Interim* (1944–55) and, reviving it in Las Vegas in 1986, continued it and recently celebrated its fiftieth birthday. It appalls me to imagine how many poems by other people Stevens must have read in his editorial career. Anyone acquainted with the workings of literary magazines knows that, although usually hard up for subscribers, such journals receive whole mailbags full of manuscripts from poets, both accomplished and would-be. I'm not sure to what extent Stevens's editorial experience may have rubbed off on his own poetry, but I suspect that it may have spurred him to excel in his own work, to take chances, to seek something better than mere polished articulations of "informed despair."

Stevens has ignored poetic fashions. This book contains a few poems written back in the 1950s, which have weathered well. As far as I can tell, all the poems escape familiar categories. They follow their own gleams, with the result that they often come at the truth from odd angles. I can't think of anyone else who could have written such a quirky, unique poem as "A Problem of Vision," whose speaker swims in the waters of time and sees fish everywhere. Inimitable, too, is "Doors," in which the speaker's remembered life is reduced to portals, and what one might find beyond them on passing through. Or see "Dead Birds," "If You Should Die," "The World Is Going to End Up in Burma," "Letter to Greece"—works completely original.

Many of the poems strike me as theatrical—in the favorable sense of the word. They people a stage with characters and set up dramatic situations: "By the

Malacca Straits," "An Evening at Home," "On Drinking Guinness Stout: Seattle," "Earthquake: Burma," "The Relay of the Cross." This element of drama in Stevens's work seems hardly coincidental. Stevens, who has written extensively on drama, is an actor good enough to have performed in summer stock, even in plays by the Bard, and to have won his director's wings.

Perhaps because Stevens has been writing poetry for such a long time, this selection displays considerable formal variety. However open and unfettered they may seem, Stevens's poems tend to fall into set line lengths, sometimes a modification of blank verse. In most cases, the ghost of meter lurks behind the arras—that benevolent spirit which, T. S. Eliot believed, haunts all competent free verse. Stevens's work ranges from the spacious freedom of "Pocatello" to the terse rhymed stanzas of "Child Before Fire," a poem cast in lines as brief as three syllables, and the similar concision of "Purcell Afternoon," a poem for his friend Virgil Thomson.

In tone as well, this collection is also long on variety. Stevens can mine a vein of wry, understated wit, as in "Today's Poet"—a portrait of an "expert on our informed despair"—and "Reading Pater in Las Vegas." If poetry, as W. H. Auden defined it, is "the clear expression of mixed feelings," then Stevens's "Cowboy Poetry Gathering: Elko" fits the definition to a T. He is capable, too, of comic introspection. "I should have died Established or at least Taboo," he remarks ("And One Other Thing"), well aware that his work has been neither banned nor universally acclaimed. In contrast, one of the most immediately appealing poems in the book, "My Dry Cleaner Branko Reads of the Shelling of Dubrovnik . . . ," captures with understated sympathy the quiet anguish of an ordinary citizen. At least as touching, in a different way, is the compassionate lyric "Interval":

> Now unfolded we are back with the dust
> I hear her gray piping from the stars
> I watch her distances her dim refrains
> Her fingers turn the pages of the light.

Luckily for us, From the Still Empty Grave is an ample selection from the whole of Wil Stevens's bold and persistent work in poetry. Perhaps it should have existed years ago, but having it before us now, we have reason at last to celebrate.

X. J. Kennedy

ITINERARY OF LOST KNOWING

How the old bustle!

ITINERARY OF LOST KNOWING

Trail toward the wide times
And the break of loud dawns
Cursing the metaphors of fire
Riding heat on sleeping children.

Our way was a well way
We drenched our shadows and our places
We read aloud our fears
And wept in all our hands.

To toy against those days' murders
All the call to rise and go
To see the sounds of now and for
And crush the trail and cut the way.

BY THE MALACCA STRAITS

In Malacca the heat was gray
Waiting rain hovered the water
The crowded cab from Kuala Lumpur
Dumped me at the bazaar.

It was lovely there and touched
By atrocious sun and steaming rice
I looked to buy a walking stick
I almost forgot to smell.

He stood through the misty light
A lithe pedicab boy watching his feet
We bargained I gave up the stick idea
He drove me to Old Church on shallow sea.

Away from the one main traffic light
Up a swing of cobblestones to Grand Hotel
Grand Hotel (there's always one) murking
Listlessly along from Conrad to the end.

This retreat stood there dying
At the end of the main hill street
Low toned Malay departed British
Inside the restaurant humming bamboo fans.

Near silence rinsed the restaurant
The fans went on with slow greed
Gyring the flies to and fro
A long high room a bar an old Chinese.

Three waiters more boys again
One put his transistor down
He ran into the kitchen laughed
The cook chased him out beer came.

I inhabited the bar alone
A Japanese girl cashier smiled up the teak
Then came the moment of encounter
I was led to table by a new presence.

Her flowing hinted at time before time
Her sandaled feet were delicious her frock maroon
Outside now the rain I heard a door
Closing on someone near and away.

I sat and the damask edged around me
Then I looked up into Asia and in ecstasy
Saw the badge brocaded on her breast
TRAINEE it said TRAINEE TRAINEE TRAINEE.

SENDING DOWN

While in Kuala Lumpur at a new green hotel
Overlooking the track where early riders run
I sent down for ice indeed didn't have
To cool my heels before it came quickly.

The bearer beautiful and young but adorned
In this century in tight western red
Trousers he made the room witness to a parade
He was that cheeky that prepared for this world.

I had been mending fences with myself
Thinking again that Asia was surely daring me
Daring me to breathe reconstitute align
Come back to what had been sleeping touched.

It was the smell the beauty of surrender keening
The right *rage* blowing through an airy pantaloon
Dung by the rivers children in hungry wonder
Vapors of old truths steaming through the vision.

Then this Malaysian Soutine bellboy walked
In carrying the ice and murmuring about Cornell
And the Hotel School there and the fine "moneez"
I caught my breath of course went back to my book.

POSTCARD: LAMB HOUSE, RUE, EAST SUSSEX
(for Henry James)

The postcard from Rye says:
"E. F. Benson leaving Lamb House
For a walk, circa 1930." Where
Is Benson going? He is just
Stepping out and there are two
Steps to the walk of the East
Sussex cobble. To his right
A dog is in the gutter it is a
Collie and it is surely defecating
To the upper right of the dog
A man is seated sketching under
The magnificent windowed quadrant
Bombed to bits in 1941 but that
Is another story for Benson
Is certainly on his way in 1930
Or circa 1930 and Henry James
Has been dead for more than fifteen
Years and the dog is dead
And we will never see the sketch
Postcards such as this do great harm
But then The Master would have approved.

RYE

The old go with the town
The pronouncement of dead fleets
Of vagabonds and pirate air
How the old bustle!

The sheep are old
They become their own pastorals
By the encroaching isthmus
Ancient dangling chatter everywhere
Battered St. Mary's by the Tower
A kiln of resurrected fires
The dead and busily dying
On the cobbles prancing playing
Toward the attendant shadows
Suavely in coming twilight
Treasures edge the sea
Bowls of golden graces.

DUET

In Taipei the egret stands by the water buffalo
In the morning paddy which lies next to the
Small factory which borders the highway
The egret is watching for the ticks
Which abound around and among the gleaming
Sweat of this fine ancient beast.

Riding by, I catch and harbor continuing looks
At the white bird standing in such quiet
Courtly loyalty in the steamy August mud
In the shoots new planted with statuesque
Pauses and steady plunges
Planters in motion bird and beast at rest.

How long the watching and waiting have been
Nobody can count but they have gone on long
Before buses prevailed the roads and the
Leap of the bird to the back that has been
A loving flap and rhythm close to forever
The entry lover waiting for the bugs to bite.

So the great beast stands in muck
Right now he controls nothing except the presence
Of such an opposite being whose plumage
In dawning shadow adorns him only
Their noble ugliness and thankless beauty
Wait out the centuries in the Chinese fields.

DEAD BIRDS

As a child he found that the bird who had died
Had no soul which he could have saved
That was his main contact with Nature
He became a teacher and fled his family
His places were cities for the most part
Cities in the night much reading fewer ladies
He kept remembering the bird and found
Sooner or later that there were never too
Many dead birds to see anywhere he pursued
The idea of the lack of dead birds
But found that he could not bring too much
Of them into his teaching the indifferent young
The books piled up in his head and city rooms
After making love he found that he bent
Over the side of the bed to catch the last paragraph
Turn the page while his current friend
Usually unread would lie whimpering
In mild and somewhat bewildered protest
The dead bird kept coming back like some
Transcendent memory eking itself out
When he looked up from his chair to stare
At the crumbs on his rug or the mist
Of letters from editors inflicted with
His poems most of them about the fear of the dead
Bird and his dead life and the sounds of strangers
Menacing the stairs in his many houses and rooms
If there had been a soul to that bird he knew he
    must
Discover it for himself which he came about
To doing when he was teaching one summer living

In the attic of a Greek professor whom he never
Saw but knew was famous and one day jarringly
And in sudden nervous anguish a bird a scarlet
    tanager
Flew in and crashed indeed impaled a moment
    against
Shirt pins inhabiting a note-filled bulletin
Board nestled above his rented desk near the curved
Window from which he would each morning curse
    each
New day he seized the bird that is he took some
Part of it and hurled it out across the roof
He watched it fall to the lawn watched it recover
And miraculously depart resurrecting in flight
The spirit of its Brazilian times and places all free
It was then that he knew that the dead bird
Of his childhood had a soul that the books
On his floor had no endings and that he himself
Would almost certainly die without fear in the
    cautious city.

ANOTHER POEM ON THE TEARING DOWN
OF THE METROPOLITAN OPERA HOUSE

Who has seen the old baritone of my childhood?
The one on Stage Left who was fat and alone
And sang Verdi as if he owned him and as if
Nobody nobody at all was around to tell him
That he was in the chorus of a tired opera
And that he was neither Milton Cross nor a lesser
   saint.

Where is the baritone of my childhood, the
Old Baritone I used to see (I think) leaving onto
The avenue and into the subway with a copy of the
News tucked away in an abused coat on a bitter night?
Once in Aïda he shook his fist at the audience
During an otherwise quiet matinee oh fine oh fine.

AN EVENING AT HOME

One story fingering the courts of native prosody
So very long ago was that at home and in his cups
Tate in the presence of his guest Cowley (also
    smashed)
Hearkened to the tortured cry of his own muse
So long suborned and haunted by the primary sly
Power of his critic's legacy this Tate this old New
    Critic
Seized upon his verses gathered in original
    manuscripts
Appropriately sanctified in books and the anointed
Quarterlies spreading the Good News through the
    Grace
Of Grants this Allen then this inebriated
    predeconstructionist
Did in conjunction with the reticent but equally
    pissed Malcolm
Commence to cremate page by page poem by poem
His efforts fortified for the gruesome task with shots
    of Old Crow.
As the victim count increased however Cowley grew
    restive.
"All, all?" he asked. "Why not save one?" for the little
    inferno
Grew steadily more minute making the proceedings
    unthinkable
The wretched Tate paused (did he hear Carolyn
    above at her beads?)
His "The Swimmer" had already joined the
    incandescent purge

"Think anthologically," Cowley pleaded. "Save one
for Cleanth."
And then the tears appeared in explicational resolve
Miraculously the ODE was the next creation sadly
destined
For the well-wrought urn was now deservedly
reprieved
"Ode to the Confederate Dead" remained in the
syllabus
Cowley from the rascally North had saved the day
Thus hushed and shamefaced sobered and
redeemed
These two old pillagers of the word retrieved
unfinished
Sonnets from the floor caressed a now-unthreatened
Villanelle and ever remorseful with bowed heads
Leaning on each other climbed their solitary way to
bed.

A PROBLEM OF VISION

Wherever God asked me to look I saw a fish
I saw a fish in my mother's teacup
I saw a guppy on the end of my niece's balloon
Actually there was a real flounder in my egg
At breakfast and a minnow in my pipe.

I say that these were real fish
God kept asking me to see and smell and not protest
But when a black crappie nibbled my napkin ring
And a sea trout taunted me at table with a shrill gill
I went along with time and thus I was hooked.

DOORS

In January the lovers fled out Le Procope
The ensuing slam like a screen door in summer
The airport door almost blew Aldous Huxley
Back on to the Western Airlines tarmac in 1960 I
    thought
Of that the night he died when Kennedy died
They held the door for Kennedy when he walked
Into the Tabernacle in Salt Lake City in 1960
The Republican prophets received the young man
Tenderly somewhat unlike the Book Depository
    door
Through which a young man walked in 1963.

The Laundro-Door Room 2617 at the Chicago Hilton
Sticks and squeaks when closing on the dirty shirts
Someone has scraped or ripped a seam in the brown
Door to the Church of St. Mary the Virgin West 46th
Street New York City where before Evensong I saw a
    woman
Crying as she walked into the Lady's Room which
    falls
Below the High Altar where the Sacrament is
    Reserved
Glass doors being shattered by wind and hard
    slamming
Include those of the Humanities Building University
Of Nevada Las Vegas the oculist's shop in the
    modern
Shopping Center (Bloomsbury) near the Russell
    Square

Tube and a storm door threatening a house in
    Pocatello Idaho.

The teak doors in Mandalay sweated and the house
    lizards
Stuck on them occasionally died like impaled hors
    d'oeuvres
In Rio a man kicked down the bathroom door of his
    flat
To find his wife in the shower with a Professor of
    Sanitary
Engineering it is true what the preachers say when
    they talk
About the Doors of Knowledge and Truth what with
    the
Subways and the omniscient elevators we
Will always open up drop down punch in faithfully
As by the main door to the great cathedral in San
    Marco
A begging dwarf always sits begging the doors never
    close.

BROOKLYN AND BROWN

Now that the digging is done
And we have mounted his tears on our slides
We can return to matters of the unborn
And the careful killing of new wonders.

A PARTICULAR TENURE

I keep seeing so many coathangers
And I smell so many rainy days
God smells galoshes in the closets
Of PS 152 and later vagrant umbrellas
Buried in the trials of waiting libraries.

Soon after the old professors die
The books come home to roost
The sign and sound of papers and voices
Start blaming the back of your mind
For not knowing that the dead were right.

FOR MONTGOMERY CLIFT

One night it was a raining Tuesday
I saw him young in Providence
In a bad bird-eye play about freedom.
My sense was then and is now
That he knew more about the play
Than the play did and that his special
Haunting of the stage came with
Coffee, some sea, and our distant fears.

SEATTLE

But dead or drunk we never reached that ship.

.

FOR A FRIEND: UPON HIS RETIRING TO THE COUNTRY FOLLOWING A WAR

In that four-year fast
Did you speak to the sea
Or find the mind
To know the field logic
Sending you epistling through
The undergrove of special fears?

With goats and games and other
Woodsy things you sit with
Fardel and with far-off love
(Now dead) now dead
And play confederate
Like a strumpet in a barn.

Is there peace in playing
Without platoon and lesser
Sycophantic glooms among the hay?

The truck boy is deceased
Like willows, library wanderers
All the "were men."

Unlearn that quoted cordwood look
And try a distance on the house.

There is always afterthought
There is always prayer.

VISITING POET

The visiting poet stands quietly
By the steps to his appointed office
He keens the ground before and behind
He considers with care the books
Embellishing the borrowed office shelves
He looks blandly at all the old professors
He thinks of old menus old restaurants
He glories in old times old taken chances
The visiting poet stands the steps
Then turns and mounts the merry-go-round
Ringing itself around the low high table.

FOR THE LEAST ONES

In cerebration and in sound
The surf is night and soft silence
Sacrament the kill of love cries
Time a drowning and a sledded spine.

Sound come and sound belie
The armature of season which ascends
And cones with grassy verity
Each rain among my trials and leaves.

> *The young cautions crease the ground*
> *The coined metallics voice the sand*
> *And Henry, horseless, loses wit*
> *In the limbo of a tired field.*

All floors are feline
All chords the mating of sigh
The tales are weary memory from
Slights of a crafty embrace in time.

Cold mountains move a cold feat
Lions lick snow in a vortexed valley
Flies die in shadows
Sticky with sun.

> *There was no moon when they left him*
> *He coughed and looned alone*
> *He shed his skin on an acre*
> *They couldn't feel the he of him.*

When we came a gill of light
Gutted the slats like mist
Some ageless numbers stalked the dust
As I kissed her eyes.

CRITIC UNDEFILED

This random blood affronts my pensive day
The unfilled gourd of hope assails my knees
I walk stone cold on streets of proper trees
I hear all children quarrel in the clay.

I hold my neutered books against the air
The treasuries of rupture shade my sun
The bells of tired insight bagged and hung
Decoy my fear and cauterize my prayer.

A saint can build a box kite with his sins
And hold his shriven pity by a string
But grounded and appeased I sorely bring
My dear dead wit to school and paint with pins.

ON DRINKING GUINNESS STOUT: SEATTLE

One night at the end of a war
We tried to swim from a partying houseboat
To an anchored schooner presiding on Portage Bay
We almost made it by bubbling crawls
We were poll-poets wogging everywhere
Our evening cachinnations were epoch
We clawed books turned instant philosophers
Made GI Bills our humming grounds.

The schooner was spawned by Irish-rich Guinness
It seemed to loll there just for our festivities
It had stayed at rest through the years of killing
It lurked in the bay's middle keeping out history
Attended by two shadowy and unallied retainers
They had hung on the side of particular war
Like sloths watching feet and sky
From the ship's bow a view a bridge singing.

I see the nights those watery years
Not often without nightmare or the song
On the bridge beyond the schooner an office-mate
Had started to retch and die crossing over also
One scholar reciting Old Norse in beery tears
At all the notions which had betrayed him started
To do his dying there oh many who really felt
The total sting entertained that murk-gloved bridge.

Looking back (again like swimming halfway under
Water to the schooner) the night was a question of
Cause (later the office-mate stuck steady in his

Way and killed himself on an alternate bay)
And the cause was varied as to new grotesques
Unremembering lovers dispossessed unknowns
Old faces turned old milk moldering
The fusty bathtub full of books.

Thus all were on the houseboat that night
And yes tails flashing a lot of us dove polluted
Toward the praying exiled sails sitting in that
Preposterous harbor unloved and neutral
We then too were unstated but unsecured
In the best kind of ignorance all mistaken
Now we all are dead separate or in wonder
But dead or drunk we never reached that ship.

IDAHO

The drowned trumpets of action
In memory chill the fires of place
Rivers and hills mix bone with stone
Tenderness fights the science of self
The lost houses tremble and tell.

THE WIND OF HILLS

Breaking through comes the wind of hills
Aware and intent upon the sullen land below
The night is ice to this wind
The sun is miser to this wind
And the people stay and stay watching their sky.

Where is the traitor in the town?
Or if there is no traitor where the clown
To make the streets glow or the wind sing?
Wind pouts down into the talk of noon
Into the talk of death on the mountains around.

A hunchback who works with thread and cloth
Walks through the wind with dead eyes
The mothers walk hurling the wind away
The children stammer with their fathers
The streets are cold with the sorrow of belief.

A dark treasure is imaged away on the mountains
A treasure is loved away on the plains
Talk often goes toward the bad cities
Or the rich green over the mountains away
From the dry river and the dead dirt lost forever.

And behind the wind is stone on stone
Stone hurling against time and against pain
Stone too old to betray or even know man
Man who fights the wind in this dark corner
Of God's mind craving the absent blessing of silence.

IDAHO

The beloved desert sits by the dry sea
And all the people pray there wonderingly,
These my strange brothers are aghast
And dull in their freedom as they watch here.

Will the greenness ever shock their feet
As they walk into the pink dusk holding
And asking the mountains to contain madness
Or the roads to bless a stranger's shoes?

I have heard the hills hurt and wonder,
I have known water to cry and be afraid,
I have seen boys and pebbles drag behind
Thunder asking how to die alone and free.

PRESENCE

The face is in the book and on the stair
The face is smoke and fear and drowning afternoon
All lying tense about the air
The face is a muddy dare asking me to breathe.

I see pages of place (God pity that act)
I assess a sane sound world of scream
For nameless saints I am a bear for thought
I count Christ by dozens through the window snow.

What violent echo hides behind my need to touch?
(In what sherry seminar did I leave my love?)
There is wood on my feet
Dread in my mother's dreams and in her hands.

The face is a holiday of why
Each time we die we hold it once
So let the fire rub on me again
God's ice is my only road.

IF YOU SHOULD DIE

If you should die in my house
I will be afraid of the wind which brought you
When they take you down the stairs unevenly
And deposit you like cotton in the car
And then take you down again to take your blood
I will know my house is not right for me.

I cannot bring you back again
And if this banal truth is true you should not die
You should not die at least in my house
Where there is a speaking tube and an old piano
And where people once sang at evenings
And where my father lay dead to receive my child
    kiss.

If you should die in my house
And if there were an ocean near my window lights
I would crawl on my roof and fly over the strapped
    thing
They use to take people like you to lower rooms
Those tax-free rooms full of silence and sirens and
    coffee
Where already I lie dead with you cold and stone
    and true.

HERE

On the way back to you
On the track of long knowing
I found ourselves lost
In the same still wilderness

On the way back to you
The markers fitful the water rare
I heard the dead Sunday aunts
Saying "Don't run away again."

The old aunts often on odd
Streets I taste the plums they
Stewed into time and talk
Like some dead log I sink.

On the way back to you
I do remember this
You dropped your shoes
On our graves and stayed listening.

On the way back to you
The watchful trees mix and attend
While I find us again
The canny aunts were right.

POCATELLO

I

Into the broken raid of feet
Running on the dawn streets
I hear my own beat and lost time
Sending shrill menaces of age
Into the wires of my fear.

The drowned trumpets of action
In memory chill the fires of place
Rivers and hills mix bones with stone
Tenderness fights the science of self
The lost houses tremble and tell.

I hold the Body in my hands
I hear rain bleeding through the roof
I watch the wood through my eyes
Windows of rain are around me
His hour is day.

II

And then the skittering morning
With mobs of *say* and *do* and *know*
Roils on campus grass with young time
I see Ned and Nadine learning to die.

> *Fold away your mind*
> *And skip skip skip*
> *Oh they'll never skip*
> *On this lost lawn.*

Tanya a queen (B)bee comes merrily
Out of a stone house of henny huns
Her teeth like Timothy's bones
Her breasts bouncing at the hills.

Even in her grave she will wander
She will never surprise at the darkness
Of this dead land holding her thighs
The ardent remnants of her half grace.

> *Tell the year around*
> *Tell the tale and die*
> *Breed among the sound*
> *Watch the new love lie.*

III

Away with them
They cavort away from Grace
And Grace itself will not do their pride
Their own land is all.

In a tenty kind of steel I greet brothers
Brothers under the rims of rented owls
Brothers a-mantis and un-amanti
Brothers unguent and flowing in their fear.

These robed civilians gather ungowned
For the morning kill (the flesh is weak)
And sing a didly-do to the subvented tryst
All tweeded for the final prayer to prey.

The unencumbered actor feels his cards
His eyes his mind his sound his gay retard
The bloated farmer chews his cud
The never-made-it hollows his hounded hint.

It takes a heap of lovin'
For the whole thing to die right.

I want to love what I was not
I want the hills to ponder germless on history
I retch between prone steel and fixed ideas
The tapering of morning is slow wonder.

High over wars and trout singing
The young are flying at seats
Making the lines raw and running
Fish and blood covering tragedy
Are mixed in a vessel of now and then.
Today the terrible father Lear persuades
O Lear is a tyrant even in this room
Lear I am coughing I am coughing I will
Not hear you bleed like this on State time
Ripeness is all unbuttoned basketball.

Five male fellows well met without bell
Two always together and wanting it
(Teachers all) one alone thinking hate easternly
The plaided coon hunter covered with Greek
Learned Jo-Jo holding skull-man looking at his
    moon.

AND THE NEW PRECIOUS TREACHERY
            THE BEARDS
        the lovely WANted ones . . .
    Ring again Mother Bell.

                    IV

I touch that steel again going down
It is new steel in unsteeled time and place
I see the hills beckoning banality and toads
I am hit by a wind and its time and loving
Its striking makes me both mad and calm
If it sets me right I will not fear
For its sound is one with me without the steel
And God himself wets my lips with an old curse.

        In the noon I will get ready to die
        In the noon I will see a friend *somewhere*
        But the pity of it is the pity's still there
        As a baby dies or dead grass burns.

These people wretched in immunity to life
Mean what they say they are not proud
They are grafted on themselves in their own shells
If a book is not bred it is not read
And the hills show them the way to a vacant sun
WE ARE LEAVING ON TRACK 2 we are gone
We are here watching a cipher die a brother born
I breathe and watch and haunt the selfish noon.

V

Let it be said we are on the edge of mountains
We are enclosed by a strange hatred
Watched over by women who have never left their
    God
We are preempted by their fear of silence
Guarded by their tentative laughter
Goaded by their breeding want of impossible beauty
Alas their exiled foals wait for each dawn
Wait on each mountain edge fearing the sea.

A man once cautioned me in a strange way
A man told me to die not knowing
That the way of the day in his time was true
Without café or urinal or tired talk or the impossible
She who fondles and does not question
I tough I touch my child and ask God swirling
Everywhere is this the tone you wish to ply
My child has no answer he is only flesh
And I am tried in this true time
To hold his teeth between his breath and help him
    die alone.

> Sorry little form you did not hate
> You were a form and not a State.

VI

Recovered afternoon what is it you pit against me
    now
Afternoon made ripe in a maze of sun

44

My boy is home spinning his hair and loving sound
He blazes this special winter time for me
My boy is heard and knows the hearing well.

One sweats a lecture as gin or heroes sweat hate
It is a steamy memory made hungry
The room ogles out a face on a small boy
And a tout from town (poodle-crapped its holy
    streets)
Sheds noise from hills on my boy's fair hair
They blow soup together behind the mortgaged
    glass.

O time in my city hands I love the window
Or the dawn I hate to see after sleep
I must fall toward mountain or rented cave to know
If the long lunch is ever over or cooked or dead
There is always a thug in my room hold still.

VII

Gracious unto the feast of me God damned
She comes and I am fearful of the wind and sound
I rest between her as a log might die
And my damp death waits out her life.

VIII

Afternoon academe whores are we
Screwed on the pages of penury
Screwed with the benefit of company
Id   Id   He.

High coffee now the polite scratch is among us
There is a clerical collar in the grounds
Hello father I sinned as you never dreamed I would
And we all are rubbish of God I cannot wait
To tell about the air I felt when getting here
My student stank a new violet in my face and quit.

I deaden back through the smiles
I smell myself and these books
As my colleagues sit on initialed chairs
And sniff for a war and say their prayers.

> He was sore on the Cross so sore
> No classical hyena saw him bleed
> No despairing frantic sees him hang
> People care for their dead in so many different ways.

IX

These hills are not the interlude but the fact
Crowing on all the glorious streets
These hills rivered made and Godded finally
Are the changing signs of my days
These hills are bearded for the Fall and tressed with
     love
They are the evening power of breathing amazed
     and in fear
These hills will always wait for me to die.
Hills changing under the treachery of my want
Gape amuck and change for the speckling nones
Of a queer flabbergasted and unreceiving silence
Hills you have corded this blunt valley long enough
The tired men are filled with you and their gain

They have sucked your guts with their pride
And these men they do not amaze at their greed
Hills there is a great sharing here always.

There is really no town no gown no hill
There is a festering of minds waiting
Wooded mirrored patient dying taken
To ravish is to know and to die
Hills I grieve for the parchment of your grace
Sanctify my lost city and my menaced son
The terror is among me and the roots unclothed
Make my sorrow plain.

X

Somewhere I have lost the green God
Somewhere a small angel tatted on me
I could be ablaze waiting for the green
But here it will not come it is buried
In downcast eyes and dust flaking every dawn.

Yet the green God is not completely gone
Even though the dust children leave
From the sea the green God counterpoints
Within some isolated creek some dull pond
Set in our migrant interloping haunt.

And the displaced stylists eating the dawn Bread
Eating Him in the land of the homemade holy clay
Their ferment germinates a silent growing Green
Which I tongue treasure and mix with whimsy
As I nod out in sly sleep in this comfortless land.

CHILD BEFORE FIRE

Slow my child
Into comfort drawn
The sky is bright
The morn is hell
And God is night
And none are well.

Slow my child
Into comfort drawn
The wood is black
And drink is cold
Yet feel no lack
For God is old.

BURMA

To move toward sound toward whispers of stillness
Toward the burden of its own time seeking rest
From death seeking a way to what was always known.

CHRIST IN BURMA

Christ came to Burma on the charger
Of old sand and new rice and sun
The people saw his face and ran
Christ came to Burma and won old air.

I saw Christ in Burma by my garden
I saw his Cross winging its wood toward me
I saw the faces on the street outside my fence
I saw Christ die in Burma by a well.

Christ came to Burma for a prayer
He came and stayed and saw a morning bird
He came and touched a peacock in its sleep
Christ kissed God in Burma for a song.

BURMA: NINE REFLECTIONS
ON AS MANY FERNS

The lattice of thought lifts evening
The Burmese night is dense
Like rain and the idea of old dust
Wit is cozy in the bruised teak room.

Breathe like air and live closely
For noon will break the chair around
Your head and you will die
Alone in a foreign fog.

But love through the lattice of this night
Lift through this strange cloud
Shout through the anger of silence
Let them know the fear.

Burma beast is a creeper on the heart
In the night air the fawn scampers
Back into the breast of self
And the rain waits cautiously.

I shout down a diadem
Waiting for the morning gray
Burma sitting on clouds of line
I wait for this miracle to eat my heart.

Cry for a chorus of one in Burma
As you cry for one sun
And you will die in the kindness
Of a holy fire you cannot find.

Dry is the dust on my ground
Burmese dust eating my heart
Again my heart in the dead dirt
O goddess of time tell me softly.

I die toward Burma alone
As it seizes my old corpse
And hurls it back into the petal
Of the flower I never touched.

Green bug Burma flying dead
In life by wild fullness
Dying everywhere caressing all
I see the grass between your eyes.

MANDALAY

The *durwan* throws the stunned banded krait
Over the compound wall then goes back
To sleep his grunts have made the baby
Cry the baby afloat upon the nanny's
Shoulder the nanny's name Teresa
Christian Madrasi wakened to surprise
In Burma Burma always the undone
The overrun the put aside the xenophobic
Its dew-filled flower hiding within
Uncertain of mercy Burma hears and sees
The creases in the land the charlatan
Deceivers in musky tribunals spitting
The betel juice coveting the temple gold
Voiding and bathing in the waiting river
Burma the reluctant the separated
Always changing places with itself.
Teresa murmurs toward her infant charge
Sometime after daybreak her garrulous
Bespectacled father pursues a chicken
To kill for the unblessed the unenlightened
The *mali* moves through the sunflowers
Above the next door the crazed Welsh diplomat
Leaves his ringed tub and blows his tea
Das (the chicken killer) has told him all
The lively early morning gossip.
A neighboring houseboy has unreasonably
Hung himself he dangles in nearby shadows
It is an unlikely improper time his dying
This gentle boy who walked without haste
And talked tenderly to small living things.

54

The banded krait has left the road
It has refused to die it balances the death
Beyond the students walk hand in hand
The headless chicken is bloodily dancing
The usual omens of flying *pongyis*
Cigars and hanging boys of Burma
In incomplete ascendancy in shimmering
Despair have taken their places among
The circles of creation.
All is at bay what new disciple will prevail?
What blessing will announce itself
Or pass away? O season of summer
Of late monsoon reveries visions unrevealed
Invocations presiding over the myth
Hear the orange monks in monotone address the
    sun
See pagodas hover the pain of the old roads.

BLAIR IN BURMA

Very often he would think back on Eton
"I might have found the whole thing out
there," he thought, "or at least suspected
what it was like here." He sat
Regarding who he was and what he
Was changing to; it was amazing to have
This brush with the inconstant spirits which
Kept hovering over him while down apace
An old man in spotted longyi stood looking
Looking knowingly at the earth.
He had found that here everything had already
Been it was no good attempting to advance
Beyond what somehow had in some
Eternity been decided and yet
There were contradictions involving power
The things so surely perceived
(An elephant, a laughing child, tears
On a morning pillow) had to be focused
Controlled this was the way it had
To be; Eton had said there must be progress
Pieces to be picked up and bought
And sold and of course there were always
People to be run in and out of life
To accommodate whatever it was that
Was happening; what was happening?
For surely Eton was wrong at least
The gongs in the temples kept reminding
Him of this; who indeed was being
Controlled? It was a sorry destiny
To have to define the Good in this way

To sit among strangers to drink alone
And then be servant to the sun; how
Would the cyclic drama of destruction
And the role of the punishing invader
Visitors be resolved? The cur dog
Following the condemned man knew
But could not say and when the thief
Having said his final crying prayers
Then hung in the shed in a turning dangle
The young policeman also knew
He had to see that the rice was
Not holy that the ground was full of paths
That led to more paths that led
To having to self and that all
This possession was supposed to be invincible
Destined to be accepted by everyone
Even the saintly monk who reputedly
Flew over the pagodas even the new
Mother washing her hair in the river
The corruption had to be for everyone
This is what he had been sent out to say
This was his sacred conflict his new history
But he was to learn that in Burmese there is
No word for dusk simply a picture which
Speaks and defines it as "when brother
Cannot recognize brother." He was to
Learn of "an-ah-deh" which means "your
Pain pains me" he was to learn that having
Supreme possession was to defile the dust
Defile the pain what a horrendous sorting
Out of cosmic clutter this terrible knowledge
Entailed this need to discover new means

Of exhortation new ways to become part
Of the redundant comedies of conquest.
And in all of the prying patterns
Where was the guilt the expiation
The expected sequences? those matters
He would have to contain he must see
The fires burning hints all around him
Somehow he must gather up the love
Around him and touch it with curious fingers
He must admit this fear not squander the offerings
He must accept the inevitable fate
Of the departure with its bruising secrets
Of knowing grace and the lasting thunder.

EARTHQUAKE: BURMA

Maung San Pe at a pensive tilt brings the tea
The bridge game under the tree beside
The house progresses while the trembling
Continues to hint of lower life wayward
Threatenings interruptions mischief
In a minor key although not too minor
For each time the trembling gestures
There are echoing sighs insistent moans
From some invisible distance beyond
The dripping leaves hanging down to dry.
"The Ava bridge is down"
The sandy tea-taster remarks reaching
For his gin "I wonder how many of them
Fell in, damned abusive thing to happen."
The cards fly by Naga the Madrasi doctor
His wife Ranjini standing touching
His shoulders she a doctor too mentions
The early morning baby she delivered
By the River where she is known as "Angel,"
And now Maung Pe and silent friends
Carry the huge teak bed into the garden
By the table after a treacherous trip
Down the stairs such stairs have no felicity
Last night next door clustered in the Consul's upper
    room
We were with Kyi Kyi as Eliza reading Shaw's
    Pygmalion
Kyi Kyi the Eliza was suffering in literacy
When the shaking started and down in piles
We fell into the garden as if pursued

Miraculous in the flowers stood cook Das with
    brandy
On a silver tray and from the next house cradled
In the arms of Teresa came the American baby
We heard the ghost on Mindon's battlements
Exacting their endless penitence
Burma had entered the imagined time
Burma in clamorous reluctance had announced
    itself
And now tonight the cardgame over the baby
    between
Us we will sleep perhaps forever in Mandalay
Maung Pe suddenly says we will drop into another
    world.
Under the net we will listen to all the secret life
The centuries will stick to us covering us
Like the gold leaf adorning
The fallen temple walls.

THE WORLD IS GOING TO END UP
IN BURMA

The world is going to end up in Burma
There with the water buffalo and the roads
The sun as hot as history
The northern rains the quakes the blessed pagoda
Worshipers there is where it will all end
In Burma with its trembling people their
Longyis sopping with monsoon their purses
Empty from monks and Chinese and every
God talking to them about the way the way
Oh it will end in Burma I promise you that
All the teak beds will moan not with love
But with crackling of the walls of the compounds
With final chorus the students will weep with rage
Be lost and the rice will die and all those outside
Coming in will join with the end of the world
In Burma where the gold leaf and the queens
And the old empires joined and died and died.

WITHOUT BURMA

Without Burma (I cannot call it Myanmar)
I had lost a place a woman a sort of being
As I dreamed it had been about to go the time
Was waiting for a signal behind the monsoon
But I kept hoping that the soldiers would stop
The tormenting and soon somehow get home
To the night fires and what little rice there was.

Now without Burma without the staying power of
    its
Bland face its face which first says nothing then starts
To move toward sound toward whispers of stillness
Toward the burden of its own time seeking rest
From death seeking a way to what was always
    known
Hallowing the good without finally seeming to
    know the way
Inch me through the still green toward my return.

BRAZIL

I see the death in her eyes in an early room.

MAID: BRAZIL

I see the death in her eyes in an early room
Her eyes wander and wonder over a morning sea
I see her frightened womb pounce mindless on
    dunes
And I hear her sigh toward her death alone and
    unfreed.

Morning girl from the spent desert looking for
    prayer
You weep and weep alone with bounty and with
    biding
You sound the sea for a special wave and you ache
You drag your despair to the shells.

Why are you weeping crying girl
You and the man and the time always hold you fair
Girl in the morning sigh you are haunting yourself
You are begging at sand and a soundless sea.

THE SEA KICKER (RIO)

A man of the city who inhabits the next flat
Arises at five arrays in American jockey shorts
And goes seriously on his way to the oceanside
Where he flexes his urgent toes in the sand.

Then this dawn dancer (a lover still warm in bed?)
After teasing his bones plunges unwarily into waves
And gesticulates wildly at the pinkening sky
Which with final craft draws him out into his day.

Later I see him through the window of his business
    car
His toes protected by proper leather his face a mask
He drives away leaving his sea perhaps his God
And descends swiftly to the plains to buy more time
        For private poetry.

ARIZONA

Love is never at odds with the winter
It hears and is one and alone.

INSOMNIA FROM THE GREAT SNOW:
   PRESCOTT

Into what strange weather-watch
(The birds attending) did we stray?
The winds constant yet faithless intimates
Sang their strange songs over our
Transitory roofs, oh these were threatening
Night ballads jettisoning our peace
Dancing unrest around the family wish.

During the nights we would scramble up secretly
Look at the streetlight and see
Oh see, it was deadly hush, still with
Wind with wind and more more snow
The feared repetition, the ruthless questioning
Of the night (and the coming day) kept
On and on its hill haunting here and now.

In the pubs it was bitter elation
Ex cathedra pronouncements were as rampant
As those hungry birds fluttering
Their ordered choreography around the
White Greek square baring its gray
Ironic and hellenic courthouse
On our western ways, wiles and weary fears.

I predict that the preachers (bless them)
Will be "grateful" for the visitation
Of this roof-shattering heartbreaking Saint.
Visions and ruminations will hold sway

Coinciding with the Manger Child.
Sins and street virtues and likely good deeds
Will also be silver sermons on Whiskey Row.

TODAY'S POET

As a poet he was terse
Never spectacular he rather
Ran with his verse and read
It well he was old in a "young"
Sort of way and survived the
Academics the Beats the Voided
The voyeurs of the little mags
The maggots of the high and
Low salons he was brisk in the
Morning he even wrote a Handbook
For Freshman Composition although
I don't think that he would have
Liked to do the exercises himself
He dug the poetry a bit better
And ultimately after a book or
Two he was invited to Washington
When the mood was right and there
He was given a medal and a cocktail
And sent to a newly independent nation
As an attaché where he was loved
And allowed to read his poetry
Through four administrations in
Two years so that when he came back
Home he was well thought of as an
Expert on our informed despair
Thus he went from Poet to public
Without the hatred of town or gown.

FOR A LADY POET GONE BUREAUCRAT

Sundry female poet friend you noisy one
God I love to see you wear that blazer hear that blast
I feel the luncheon look and knowing smile when
We are at table together in the hinters and haunters
I love you constantly though on the run I cannot
Find you in the motel nor by the pool I keep
Finding your files everywhere and want to bring
Them to you but people keep saying that you have
Already left for Syracuse to address a rally or
Spring some poor assistant professor who cruised
And picked up fuzz by mistake and almost lost
His Guggenheim really honey I have a poem I want
You to hear not the one you said was "putrid" in La
   Grande
Nor the one you said was "too titty" in El Paso
I mean the one about us when the houseboat almost
   sank
And you decided then and there that you would
   never
Laugh again and the water around us seemed to die
And we went away and came upon all these our
   foolish ways.

WOOD WALK

To gather the wood with a hard eye
The visual thing in the sun
This is making the major remark
Pulling gently from the earth
Fitting idea into the hand
Listening for what is seen
This is to gather the real ruins
The remnants of all tugs-of-war
Walk around the tutelary mountain
Really touch then carry
Really touch wood have a land
Talk alone see the lovely cold air.

THE NEW GARDEN

Holding high the late flower of light
I propose earth for the dead
And for trees beckoning wild and alone
I ask blindness for the public man.

Where the furtive drifts of sun dwell
There is the odyssey of the coming plan
And the plan is death even in Eden
And Eden is scurrying land asking grace.

I ask love for frightened children of stars
Ranking themselves in the breeze of shadows
Praying that heavens be blind to black wisdom
Of mind and the coming comets of sky.

DRESS INFORMAL

We hear the song by the green well
A bird dies by cat the sun sets
The valley comes up through light
We are transfixed by growing death
A box in the corner of the room
Has more to say than the sun rising
This seductress this Nature is a ploy
Back and forth between things and grass
Each our constant enemy.

TO STOP SMOKING MY SON CHEWED

Having drunk my son's spit
From the shiny antique spittoon
My cat
(Named Milton)
Leapt
Toward Heaven.

PURCELL AFTERNOON
(for *Virgil Thomson*)

The lights dimming
The afternoon real sun
Hot and bright
The dare is love
The body breathing
The truth known
Such is a chord
Oh I wish to hold
You mute as the dead
Princess lying radiant
The fawn day dying.

ON HEARING THE CHOIRBOY SING
AT A STRANGER'S FUNERAL

I blessed the house in the far wood
Near where I wanted to die among friends
And where I felt the stream would always
Flow by and the hills cover us all always.

I blessed this house without appraising
Ever the day which brought it there or
The people who had loved me who made the
House and would oddly make it mine.

Blessings on things are nebulous gestures
In past times of fear and unknowing
And yet the blessings make the time.
This house my house will always stand.

AND ONE OTHER THING

I should have died a Trojan or a Spartan
Or someone mechanical or full of deadly machines
I keep seeing the more morbid side of things
When you get right down to it really
I should have been a headwaiter or a good lover
Or a Chairman preferably of someone else's Board
I keep wondering—perhaps a quiet doctor
Charging a lot and never saying much.

I should have died Established or at least Taboo
Instead I leave my card and shun the Out-of-Doors
And wonder why I should have died not being
That very Thing I should have been whether
Secluded in some New Hampshire village waging
Wisdom or perhaps wondering bitter things
Oh so sullen Things in a desert someplace where
I would have died complete and whole and all alone.

ALL WILL BE WELL IN THE WINTER

All will be well in the winter
When the streets are calm and dark
All will be well in the winter
With the sleep of the bear and the lark.

I hate no more in the winter
Its silence immense and unknown
Love is never at odds with the winter
It hears and is one and alone.

MISSOURI

I do not say I came home to earth
I say I paused and heard my wonder burn.

CALENDAR FOR WORSHIP

Indeed the day ahead had died
I was impaled on a Missouri hill
Not moving to the Protestant plain
But cuckolded by a Plymouth (Fury) on joyless ice.

I do not say I came home to earth
I say I paused and heard my wonder burn
This was Ash Wednesday the time mentioned
Time of my snow and my mortality.

POEM FOR MY SON

The land is dry and dry
The sullen ears receive your cries
The kind betrayal spawns its nebulae
Your tearing makes my wisdom bleed.

Dear son the remnants of your tent
Are swept away with dinner crumbs
You are brought to pain on wheels
A history dies upon a towel.

Dear son so nightly wrung from time
Affront my brain with your untutored grace
Your eloquence bewilders sound and sense
Your comely wounds are mine in wondrous trial.

SLEEPER FROM KANSAS CITY

The processional of the great station is long
And I tread the profound aisle toward the exit
Through to the platform down to another going
Down to other steps into safety and night Amen.

Here I am in the text of another journey
Into the gloss of another caged neighbor
I think to read and hear him over the rails
Over each division point and prayer.

Always it is a dreamed hymn of leaving and arrival
My hazy half-stagger up a new morning alley
Makes me ready to dare anew to cast about
For the next lost glove on the great station's floor.

LAS VEGAS

There was an unending riot of sorts.

VEGAS: A FEW SCRUPLES

Under scrutiny of hills in the hot sun
A woman crazed has cut her lover
Hacked at his privacies kicked
Glass at him broken glass is the thing
Here where the children at the lower
Elementary levels have one of the best
Systems and more daysleeping parents
Than Monaco it's a tight town
Full of churches rampant cars like
Pimples mapping the alleys behind
The Strip a wonderment of sullen searchers
Planted firmly on the shifty earth looking.

When Brigham sent his band here
He did not foresee what the sun could
Do but burn for the Faith it does burn
Indeed burn right for the Saved of which
There are many species transient and nested
And too there are the lesser breeds the manic
The levitated professors who floated
Into this crude escrow like bad seeds vagrant
Talent dumped from the more thoughtful cities
All sorts of burning bushes in dry tide
Now by gardens and pools the natives half watch
The cuffed change girl shuffle to the cool blue car.

MY DRY CLEANER BRANKO READS OF THE SHELLING OF DUBROVNIK IN THE *NEW YORK TIMES*

How hard this tragedy by the sea has hit him
He stands and serves within the steam
Recently from hospital (knives into the
Pituitary) he is back now to his country's terror
He shakes his head goes back to the Singer
So many buttons off the pants of the world
"Hey Doc," he says, "this is so terrible"
The customers (dealers for the black pants
Pit bosses for the striped shirts) pile
Into Branko's morning more dead children
Are invading the pages in mute show and tell
I should not have reminded him he presents
A smile as a hushed girl leaves with her leotards
Then his Greek priest with a bunch of surplices
"Dubrovnik," Branko asks, "Why in God
They do that?" the pressing the steam
The incessant hiss goes on clothing the day.

PARADISE CREST

The pit boss wives and a few other lady
Connections parade their ways together
Urgently marching their arms
Talking and testing the early sun
Occasionally a drained man will pass them
Puffing his way toward eternity
It is hard on my bones to watch them
Grouping buzzing somehow they look
So confident so proud of something
They seem to have found while over my oatmeal
I wonder what that treasure may be
These pilgrims seem to be importuning an answer
To a prayer they look as if they've
Been pimping for the recent dawn "Amazing"
I think I hear one varicose Brunhilde cry
Slapping firmly her entrenched purple
Walking shorts as she flips her cigarette
Into a pansy patch nodding at her then the
Neighbor neurosurgeon appears tugged by "Angel"
His straining pitbull the shifts keep changing
All this before seven the TWA wife happily joins one
Babbling troop her husband when not
Flying to Amsterdam works religiously on a yellow
Chris Craft now the high roller's son
Is picked up for private school two good neighbors
From work in Boylesque depart their
Porsche quarreling the Mormon Bishop zings along
Waving the truck of Mexican *campesinos* (four in
Front) negotiate the confident promenades
They too have come to greet the streets of Paradise.

BOY

Where do you walk in the tall tall grass
Where do you eat plums when the silence comes
Does your mind murmur in the long school hall
Where are your treasures and who tells your time?

You batter the sun with your raucous cries
You pick live flowers then help them grow
You can't tie your laces you don't say prayers
You breed your own thunder you hide in the house.

Deep in your wonder you've lost the true count
You bellow you bleat you turn the lights out
You make your own moonlight you sail your own
   ark
You sit counting stones in the unclothed dark.

READING PATER IN LAS VEGAS

A different kind of corrupt desert here
The High Table is moving with lots of standing
Up for meals at odd hours shouts shouts
In the night and broken glass not solitary toasts
Held for a perfect moment crystal and clear
Here is monumental spinoff from certain matters
Pater tracked toward while attacking Coleridge
Items yes about Absolute and Time
About how still the Absolutes seem to reign
Here before Keno the child goes nickel and
Hair ribbon shiny to Sunday School indeed
Another Joseph finishes his prunes puts on his
Dunes badge and leaves for Baccarat the Lord
Assenting oh Marius Epicurean could not protest.

INTERVAL

After she read about the world
My lover never sold her dictionary
She watched the dawning of words
And visited me becomingly aware.

I heard her sounds of love and wonder
Her flute relayed the choices of her hours
She held court for our final sad song
In stubborn grief we parted like two shells.

Now unfolded we are back with the dust
I hear her gray piping from the stars
I watch her distances her dim refrains
Her fingers turn the pages of the light.

HAVING IT MADE

In the next office my weekday neighbor types
No doubt about it he writes "solid" things
On Saturday mornings my beleaguered fellows
Fertile householders all saw cut mow
Water plane build Christ I am jealous
Amazed snarling angry at the noisy fuss
Why must they raise time to a boil?
This earnest rhythm this biased salute to day
Annuls my purposes as yet undefined
Indoors and outdoors constructive umbrage
Goes on while I sit thinking of unborn radishes
My stubborn bed of half-life mocking me
I hear my neighbors hear all their machines
Drilling for gold slamming my doors.

TO MY CAT DRINKING FROM THE
SWIMMING POOL

Don't.

All sorts of things
Have happened to those
Who drink
From troubled waters.

Come into the house
Drink from your bowl
Take your chances
Indoors.

THE NIGHT SAMMY DAVIS JR. COULDN'T
GO ON (LAS VEGAS)

I am still astonished
Years ago he danced with his uncle
And with his father in Seattle
He imitated Cary Grant
The world ran through him
He jumped on sixteen feet
Played the flute with his toes
Then I read that he wouldn't open
This time in Las Vegas the strike was on
The music was cold
Sammy had to sit things out
The night couldn't wake up
The bones were willing
But no tone poems to play with
Sammy couldn't run walk or sing
Oh how still a room can get
When the cats are quiet.

MEMORANDUM

Appended you will find my heart
Stapled by an assortment of ideas
And a desire to please
The enclosed is also supported
By something we recently said
Although I cannot remember
Exactly what I do recall the date
Subsequent to committee action
And contingent upon history
I will let love enter in perhaps
With full approval but this however
Depends on budget which is still
Transitory still uncommitted
Nevertheless the outlook is not
Entirely bleak since surplus funds
A due amount of courage and the
Passage of time should clarify any
Confusions or inconsistencies
Which occurred in previous committee
Action I can assure you that intense
Attention is being paid to this
Matter and that on Death's Day
(Tentatively scheduled) we shall all
Convene for books to be balanced
And for hearts to be broken and revealed.

THE FAILURE OF THE BIRDS

Most of the birds failed
In terms of bringing the right message
To the flocks of ever-assembling people
There was an unending riot of sorts.

The scholars were misconstrued and puzzled
Rivers ran the sun seemed out of time
The merchants were not at ease things leaked
But it was the birds whose songs devolved.

Toward the end as the children tried to sleep
There was some trembling of the walls some
    tempest
Busily improvising on certain death while
The birds never losing face silenced and folded.

HEARING THE VOICES

The cheap drum set presides
Over his abandoned scattered room
The visible inventory stammers
A threat to his keening solitude.
On the gaping desk rejected books
Except for Sidney Omarr on Aquarius
A green model spitfire made in "there"
And brought home on pass
For one infested try at freedom
Tape decks a glasses case (the glasses
Crushed he never wore them) a dead Palm
Saved from an unblessed Sunday
His own initialed pewter cup
Full of black spit he still asks
For gifts of Copenhagen to chew
While he listens quietly three
Pictures of the one named Kitty dark
And musing found with him in the Phoenix
Bus station the Stones upon the cork walls
His dead mother's picture by the stereo
Two dumbbells a scrawled letter to himself
Titled "My Future Focus" two tennis rackets
"AC/DC" poster McEnroe over the bed Gerulaitis
Covering the hole his head made in the door.

Today he is sixteen
I strike the cymbal
He is gone
He has taken the voices with him.

COWBOY POETRY GATHERING: ELKO

Cowboy let it out
In front of the dudes
But do you really mean it?
I look at you on Idaho Street
All gussied up deftly
Shyly treasuring yourself
Resting on the winter winds
Your trixy or faithful women
Arranging themselves
In pickups wan motels
Even the "better" Stockmans or Commercial
Anyway you recite and hold court
Have a fling with your own kind of Muse
With your own kind of horse.

The horse is the thing old friend
Even though you have never addressed
"My Kingdom," "Barberry," "St. Mawr"
Nor relished the presuming nags of a Johnny
Longden No your horse is more the lover
The means to join in and take it all
That is why you're a certain sort
A special breed of poet pardner
Your horse conjoins the new and old money
You have both become the Foundations'
Darlings you're trotting on Humanities
Riding fence on a new kind of circuit
I could almost swear you believed all that horseshit
As you invade Elko from the Tuscarora wilds.
But I'm not ever going to give you away

I like your flashy gingham and silk
The hat on the Stockmans bar beyond envy and
   despair
I like your weathered women too
Except they're not weathered anymore
They get off the range long enough
To do mischief and appropriate poems
Of their own that provide a kind of justice
For the places that they leave that's
It this poetry comes from seasonal parting
From the forsaken elements the cattle soon-to-bleed
These create Old Slim Old Sam Old Melody Ma
Cowboy you recite belief in unrecoverable myth and
   death
Your doggerel is the truth and you've come home.

THE MAN WITH THE PAPER HAT

Every campus has one
Sample good Campus Charlie
Flashing the sorority window
Just before the Supper Sing
His trench coat epaulets
Also dangling in the Seattle shade
Of Buster in Pocatello howling
Outside the Pharmacy Building
Competing with laboratory
Dogs berating their own captivity
Consider the punker monk in Gunnison
The dozens of muttering hall wanderers
Scolding themselves at Baylor
Ball State the furnace room at Brown
For me though it is triumphantly
The man with the paper hat who begoggled
Keeps appearing has majored often
Without triumph in twelve different
Disciplines whose newspaper Nelson hat
Threatens and reminds us as the black
Bike skirmishes the desert campus
Mopping up our expectations
Assaulting our morning certainty
Taking us all for a ride.

THE RELAY OF THE CROSS

The boy found the Cross in an alley
Near a cul-de-sac close to the Flamingo
And he brought It to his father
Who was a pit boss and the pit boss
Gave It to his girlfriend who was
On graveyard and who had never had
Too much time for the Cross even so
She kept It in her dance bag (she
Had wanted to be a dancer) by her
Bed where she and the pit boss went
Occasionally all the way together
His mouth in after-dew wagging about
His son crying in his sleep and hearing
Bells and they discussed this their
Cigarettes waving the whole thing off
Into the vented air which divided them
From the true stars which were watching
Them all the time watching them
And the Cross hidden from them so far
Eternally in the black dance bag
Still the pit boss thing had to end
And the girl gave up dealing she also
Lost the dance bag in a bus station
On her way to Seattle where she had
Decided to marry an anthropologist
And have a baby in a bag on her back
And buy two-pound jars of peanut butter
At discount stores though she did not
Forget about the Cross in the dance bag
And wondered about its destiny

Actually the Cross (along with three
Condoms a compact and some chewing
Gum) made it to Iowa City with a fired
Craps dealer who had shingles and a chance
To go back home to study creative
Writing with people who made a living
Loving the Cross or beating off on It
Depending on their cultural predilections
Which were various and rarely profound
As the craps dealer learned although
He was forgetful and left the Cross
In one of his many rented rooms
Left It to become a paperweight
For an old Jew not a special old Jew
Just a Senior Citizen spending his
Dying years rereading and retreating
When they found the old Jew dead
And smiling they threw most of his stuff
Out including the Cross It landed
In an alley near the library
To be picked up carted away burnt
Very probably It was not passed on.

JOURNEY

When the telephone rang
In the elevator
I was going up fast
No time to answer the phone
Just time to stand
Eyes like wondering pansies
Listening those rising seconds
To the arbitrary detestable
Chirruping shitful scratch
On my day "Why didn't
You answer it?" I was asked
Later when I had arrived up
Out and not free
Still edging back from my
Memory of the doors which had
Deposited me in a whirl
Into the autopsy-colored hall
Where the sign said
"Pick up your cards
For English 203 to your Left"
And I was not yet over
The fact of the phone let alone
My failure to open the little
Low door where it was and say
Say what? I had nothing to
Say to or on the phone
I did not ask to be
Telephoned they shouldn't have
Suggested I answer it
It was not fair of it to ring

I had hurt nobody that morning
And I was alone in that lift
They laughed when I said
The telephone rang in the
Elevator it made a good
Set of intervals between
The john the bad complexions
In English 102 the constant
Southern Baptist picnic
In the Secretarial Persons'
Workroom the weekend hangover
Recovery of a man who bit his
Nails and wrote about Thomas
Carew's Clap my telephone
Call won over Carew's Clap
Or was the call a Call for me
From the outside from some
Party of which I was the Devil
Should I have stooped down
And taken up the phone?
Would I have been found when
The door opened at Floor Six
Lying there listening to what
Had already been decided
Finally on Floor Two some
Definite design already drawn
Up for me to know God though
For me it was better I think
That I didn't know if indeed
A purpose knit those interrupting
Rings and touched me on Three
Anointed me on Four

Riveted me on Five
Pursued me to Six
Now unsustained on Six
Imperiled by that parlous
Trip that imprisoning review
Of uncabled determinations
I know this surely
If the beastly thing
Ever rings again let
Them let them answer it.

ARLEN
(for *Arlen Collier*)

The West is an idea of being away
So that one has to look at it from afar
Let us not quibble about the fact
That he searched and found and returned to tell us
He brought back the treasures so very
Unceasingly that we could not but fail
To miss some of the gems
Some of the tones of the touches some
Of the sweet balances of poised reveries
And yet we have still managed
To receive more than just an abundance of what
His death-embraced discoveries awarded to us.

Strangely my love for him was based on knowing
Knowing that I was constantly failing in hidden
Promises which through gentle intimation he
    wanted
Me to define "Oh yes," he kept reminding me
"That is the way it was, you know that, don't
You?" oh yes I knew but I also knew that somehow
He knew much more his silences confirmed that
The raciest doubt the most reliable glance
The most bland affirmation had to be judged with
    purity
Before they disappeared his dying heart insisted on
    that
So I have luckily touched his fingers in our common
    sorrow
I will keep retrieving his magnitude his water upon
    the desert.

HANDS ON

The polite boy in the Cubs T-shirt
Tells me he is a "Hands On" person
But that his father says he has to have
"This paper" so here he is poised abashed
Sitting in my office asking for help.

"Hands On!" I think and feel my own despair
I know I might not help him for I am not
A Hands On I've missed too much out there
And now before me this puzzled kid my new friend
Inquires about the cause of Lear's madness.

LETTER TO GREECE

. . . and love to you and the watching sea
From the still empty grave.

LETTER TO GREECE

Dear Kenneth far away in Greece
I should be watching Claude Rains
And Fay Wray in *The Evil Mind*
On cable and made in 1934 I keep
Wondering what they thought about
While making that movie when I
Was busy singing funerals at St.
Paul's Church Flatbush and being
Skipped half of the fifth grade at PS
152 because of teacher Mrs. Blum
At whose funeral incidentally I was
Also to sing along with Albert Turner
Who was later killed at Anzio.
But enough about *The Evil Mind*
The Cable schedule only gave
It two stars anyway what I really
Need to do is reply to yours of New Year's
Day which was a great letter
Like most of your letters you answered
The right questions although you never
Really did accommodate (indeed I never
Asked you to) the question that stumps me.
HOW DO YOU GET A GOOD FIRST LINE?
As in a proper Mormon Temple Wedding
I want to be sealed with an answer
To that one it gets more and more
Confusing I suppose you might say
That the question itself is the best first
Line (HOW DO YOU GET A GOOD FIRST LINE?)
Perhaps the question is the answer HOW DO YOU

GET A GOOD FIRST LINE? I thought
Of taking the problem down
A floor in my building to Philosophy
(The Foreign Language Ladies also live there
Stirring their convulsive Franco-Prussian
Stew.) There on Five in subdued retreat the
Philosophers hang out but they're too upset
For my concerns. Nice neglected
Valiant people some of them but too
Close to the fire so Zilch to Five
And back up to Six and the English
"Lounge" with its maggoty ice box
Its mail cubbies full of perfidy. We're
Lousy with first lines here and not just
For poetry, mostly first lines for grant
Applications and forms for winning prizes.
One of my colleagues does sturdy in-house
Publishing describing how good he
Is God he counts and courts the ways.
Not only is he good I guess, but
The people who think he's good
Have to testify in writing too and that
Takes away a lot of time when you think
Frighteningly of the national scene.
Of course our drinking buddy Ted Roethke
Did it you remember it's a wonder
He ever got any poetry done oh well
As Manny at my deli says Let's All Praise
High Seriousness. See what looking
For a good first line can do although
Come to think of it maybe I found the ultimate first
    line

My local doctor talked Hemingway while probing
Me and I told him about a show girl
At the Lido who read Bakhtin. Suddenly he
Stopped talking and time ran so that soon
I was in L.A. oh how a urological enclave
Takes you down a trifle from grants and prizes.
Minor poets my ass that was my man's
Major interest and he was Mr. Prostate
Himself, but let us to the waiting first line.
You're drunk of course when they
Bring you down rather nice drunk actually
The chattering Performers-in-Charge in their
Green frocks gathered in happy clusters
Away from the twelve (like with
The disciples) blobs on gurneys
All awaiting entrance to their twelve
Respective operating theaters it was
Noisily pleasant with the urgency
Of one of the better Fire Island parties I
Once attended with a dancer (he now
Also dead with Miss Blum) I could
See my "man" in the distance but lost
Him when She came to me Korean
Lovely almond to be had in a vapor
Worthy of gentle balmy force such
Eyes to be licked hovering mouth
Sweet to smell end of the chapter
Of a naughty book but gentle again
I now and forever remember her special
English and the needle shyly revealed.
She got close to my ear. As I felt
Her she said "You will have a very

Small prick," and then a sad
Looking Punjabi wheeled me to glory.
Was this the last line I was ever
To hear or the first line that I now
Can use? I send it to you in Athens.
I remember your fine cat Wilfred
Indeed believe I thought of him
When I came to in L.A. "God, you're a mess,"
The young nurse said as he changed my
Bandages. I wanted to kiss his fingers.
He seemed the David at the Academia in Florence
Well so much for good first or last lines.
Last Christmas I trimmed a live Mondell
Pine it's planted outside showing new
Growth I am blessed by its special presence.
I see that Channel 18 is repeating *The Evil Mind*
At 2 "Ciao" and love to you and the watching sea
From the still empty grave.

ACKNOWLEDGMENTS

Most of the poems in this book have appeared in the publications listed below. The author is grateful to many editors:

Perspective
Western Humanities Review
Quest (India)
Colorado Quarterly
Inland
The Literary Review
San Francisco Review
Brigham Young University
    Studies
Inscape
Impetus
Plainsong
Intermountain
Poetry Northwest
The Park Journal
Descant
Folio
Wisconsin Review
Twigs IV
Satire Newsletter
Pembroke Magazine
Loon
The New Quarterly
Fern
Poetry Magazine
Poetry Nippon (Tokyo)
Raspberry

St. Andrew's Review
Halcyon
Welter
The MacGuffin
Comstock Quarterly
Northern New England Review
Interim
Orbis (London)
The Signal
Blue Unicorn
Copula
Webster Review
Petroglyph
Bellowing Ark
Exquisite Corpse
Arts Alive
Curled Wire Chronicle
Bristlecone
Southern Humanities Review
Orbis
Poetry Northwest
Blackbird
The Sunset Palms Hotel
Embryo
Syncline
San Jose Studies

Some of the poems in this book have also been reprinted in *Poetry of the Desert Southwest*, edited by James E. Quick, Baleen Press, 1973; *Modern Poetry of Western America*, edited by Clinton E. Larson and William Stafford, Brigham Young University Press, 1975; *Desert Wood: An Anthology of Nevada Poets*, edited by Shawn Griffin, University of Nevada Press, 1991. "Pocatello" was reprinted through the Antioch Press in pamphlet form for the *Literary Review*, 1965. "The Relay of the Cross" appeared originally in *Seven Nevada Poets*, edited by William Fox, Rainshadow Editions, University of Nevada, 1991. Some poems in this volume were published in *The World Is Going to End Up in Burma*, by A. Wilber Stevens, Hardwood Books, 1988 and 1989.

INDEX OF TITLES AND FIRST LINES

Entries in italic are titles of poems; all other entries are
first lines of poems.

A different kind of corrupt desert here, 93
A man of the city who inhabits the next flat, 66
A Particular Tenure, 21
A Problem of Vision, 15
After she read about the world, 94
All will be well in the winter, 80
All Will Be Well in the Winter, 80
An Evening at Home, 13
And One Other Thing, 79
*Another Poem on the Tearing Down of the Metropolitan Opera
House*, 12
Appended you will find my heart, 98
Arlen, 109
As a child he found that the bird who had died, 10
As a poet he was terse, 71

Blair in Burma, 56
Boy, 92
Breaking through comes the wind of hills, 35
Burma: Nine Reflections on as Many Ferns, 52
By the Malacca Straits, 4

Calendar for Worship, 83
Child Before Fire, 48
Christ came to Burma on the charger, 51
Christ in Burma, 51
Cowboy let it out, 101
Cowboy Poetry Gathering: Elko, 101
Critic Undefiled, 29

Dead Birds, 10
Dear Kenneth far away in Greece, 113
Don't, 96
Doors, 16
Dress Informal, 75
Duet, 9

Earthquake: Burma, 59
Every campus has one, 103

For a Friend: Upon His Retiring to the Country Following a War, 25
For a Lady Poet Gone Bureaucrat, 72
For Montgomery Clift, 22
For the Least Ones, 27

Hands On, 110
Having drunk my son's spit, 76
Having It Made, 95
Hearing the Voices, 100
Here, 39
Holding high the late flower of light, 74
How hard this tragedy by the sea has hit him, 90

I am still astonished, 97
I blessed the house in the far wood, 78
I keep seeing so many coathangers, 21
I see the death in her eyes in an early room, 65
I should have died a Trojan or a Spartan, 79
Idaho, 36
If You Should Die, 38
If you should die in my house, 38
In cerebration and in sound, 27
In January the lovers fled out Le Procope, 16
In Malacca the heat was gray, 4
In Taipei the egret stands by the water buffalo, 9
In that four-year fast, 25

In the next office my weekday neighbor types, 95
Indeed the day ahead had died, 83
Insomnia from the Great Snow: Prescott, 69
Interval, 94
Into the broken raid of feet, 40
Into what strange weather-watch, 69
Itinerary of Lost Knowing, 3

Journey, 106

Letter to Greece, 113

Maid: Brazil, 65
Mandalay, 54
Maung San Pe at a pensive tilt brings the tea, 59
Memorandum, 98
Most of the birds failed, 99
My Dry Cleaner Branko Reads of the Shelling of Dubrovnik in the
    New York Times, 90

On Drinking Guinness Stout: Seattle, 30
On Hearing the Choirboy Sing at a Stranger's Funeral, 78
On the way back to you, 39
One night at the end of a war, 30
One night it was a raining Tuesday, 22
One story fingering the courts of native prosody, 13

Paradise Crest, 91
Pocatello, 40
Poem for My Son, 84
Postcard: Lamb House, Rue, East Sussex, 7
Presence, 37
Purcell Afternoon, 77

Reading Pater in Las Vegas, 93
Rye, 8

Sending Down, 6
Sleeper from Kansas City, 85
Slow my child, 48
Sundry female poet friend you noisy one, 72

The beloved desert sits by the dry sea, 36
The boy found the Cross in an alley, 104
The cheap drum set presides, 100
The durwan throws the stunned banded krait, 54
The face is in the book and on the stair, 37
The Failure of the Birds, 99
The land is dry and dry, 84
The lattice of thought lifts evening, 52
The lights dimming, 77
The Man with the Paper Hat, 103
The New Garden, 74
The Night Sammy Davis Jr. Couldn't Go On (Las Vegas), 97
The old go with the town, 8
The pit boss wives and a few other lady, 91
The polite boy in the Cubs T-shirt, 110
The postcard from Rye says, 7
The processional of the great station is long, 85
The Relay of the Cross, 104
The Sea Kicker (Rio), 66
The visiting poet stands quietly, 26
The West is an idea of being away, 109
The Wind of Hills, 35
The world is going to end up in Burma, 61
The World Is Going to End Up in Burma, 61
This random blood affronts my pensive day, 29
Today's Poet, 71
To gather the wood with a hard eye, 73
To My Cat Drinking from the Swimming Pool, 96
To Stop Smoking My Son Chewed, 76
Trail toward the wide times, 3

Under scrutiny of hills in the hot sun, 89

Vegas: A Few Scruples, 89
Very often he would think back on Eton, 56
Visiting Poet, 26

We hear the song by the green well, 75
When the telephone rang, 106
Where do you walk in the tall tall grass, 92
Wherever God asked me to look I saw a fish, 15
While in Kuala Lumpur at a new green hotel, 6
Who has seen the old baritone of my childhood? 12
Without Burma, 62
Without Burma (I cannot call it Myanmar), 62
Wood Walk, 73

WESTERN LITERATURE SERIES

Western Trails: A Collection of
Short Stories by Mary Austin
selected and edited by
Melody Graulich

Cactus Thorn
Mary Austin

Dan De Quille, the Washoe
Giant: A Biography and
Anthology
prepared by Richard A.
Dwyer and Richard E.
Lingenfelter

Desert Wood: An Anthology of
Nevada Poets
edited by Shaun T. Griffin

The City of Trembling Leaves
Walter Van Tilburg Clark

Many Californias: Literature
from the Golden State
edited by Gerald W. Haslam

The Authentic Death of
Hendry Jones
Charles Neider

First Horses: Stories of the
New West
Robert Franklin Gish

Torn by Light: Selected Poems
Joanne de Longchamps

Swimming Man Burning
Terrence Kilpatrick

The Temptations of St. Ed and
Brother S
Frank Bergon

The Other California: The Great
Central Valley in Life and
Letters
Gerald W. Haslam

The Track of the Cat
Walter Van Tilburg Clark

Shoshone Mike
Frank Bergon

Condor Dreams and Other
Fictions
Gerald W. Haslam

A Lean Year and Other Stories
Robert Laxalt

Cruising State: Growing Up in
Southern California
Christopher Buckley

The Big Silence
Bernard Schopen

Kinsella's Man
Richard Stookey

The Desert Look
Bernard Schopen

Winterchill
Ernest J. Finney

Wild Game
Frank Bergon

Lucky 13: Short Plays about
Arizona, Nevada, and Utah
edited by Red Shuttleworth

The Measurable World
Katharine Coles

Keno Runner
David Kranes

TumbleWords: Writers Reading
the West
edited by William L. Fox

From the Still Empty Grave:
Collected Poems
A. Wilber Stevens